# WOMEN OF THE
# FUR TRADE
## FRANCES KONCAN

PLAYWRIGHTS CANADA PRESS
TORONTO

For professional or amateur production rights, please contact:
Colin Rivers at Marquis Entertainment
PO Box 47026, Eaton Centre, Toronto, ON M5B 2P9
416-960-9123 X 223 | info@mqlit.ca

LIBRARY AND ARCHIVES CANADA CATALOGUING IN PUBLICATION
Title: Women of the fur trade / Frances Koncan.
Names: Koncan, Frances, author.
Description: A play.
Identifiers: Canadiana (print) 20220222304 | Canadiana (ebook) 2022022238X
   | ISBN 9780369103505 (softcover) | ISBN 9780369103512 (PDF)
   | ISBN 9780369103529 (HTML)
Classification: LCC PS8621.05825 W66 2022 | DDC c812/.6—dc23

Playwrights Canada Press operates on land which is the ancestral home of the Anishinaabe Nations (Ojibwe / Chippewa, Odawa, Potawatomi, Algonquin, Saulteaux, Nipissing, and Mississauga), the Wendat, and the members of the Haudenosaunee Confederacy (Mohawk, Oneida, Onondaga, Cayuga, Seneca, and Tuscarora), as well as Metis and Inuit peoples. It always was and always will be Indigenous land.

We acknowledge the financial support of the Canada Council for the Arts, the Ontario Arts Council (OAC), Ontario Creates, and the Government of Canada for our publishing activities.

To Louis Riel, the Mr. Brightside of the
Province of Manitoba.

*Women of the Fur Trade* was first produced by the Royal Manitoba Theatre Centre, at the Tom Hendry Warehouse, Winnipeg, from February 27 to March 14, 2020, with the following cast and creative team:

Marie-Angelique: Kathleen MacLean
Cecilia: Elizabeth Whitbread
Eugenia: Kelsey Kanatan Wavey
Louis Riel: John Cook
Thomas Scott: Toby Hughes

Director: Audrey Dwyer
Lighting Design: Hugh Conacher
Sound Design: Daniel Roy
Set and Costume Design: Linda Beech
Dramaturg: Lindsay Lachance
Fight Director: Kristen Sawatzky
Apprentice Director: Chelsey Grewar
Stage Manager: Margaret Brook
Apprentice Stage Manager: Zoë Leclerc-Kennedy

# SETTING

Eighteen hundred and something something.
A room in a fort on the banks of the Reddish River.

# CHARACTERS

*Marie-Angelique*
Métis Taurus

*Cecilia*
British Virgo

*Eugenia*
Ojibwe Sagittarius

*Thomas Scott*
Irish Capricorn

*Louis Riel*
Métis Libra

# NOTES

All hail the mighty backslash indicating dialogue overlap.
It is very wise, and it looks like this:

/

# ONE

*We are somewhere. It's dark.*

*There are three rocking chairs and not much else.*

*There are walls, however, which are covered in portraits of men: famous men, infamous men, nobody men, somebody men, men without hats, men with brooms, men who sold the world, men who fell to Earth, men of the fur trade, men of all kinds, men all over the place—just like in real life.*

*There is also a floor, as is often the case. It's an odd sort of floor and somewhere someone is making some tea.*

*And then three women enter. And they wear fur coats.*

*And they sit in their rocking chairs. And they, once again, begin their lives.*

MARIE-ANGELIQUE: In 2006, when Suri Cruise and Shiloh Jolie-Pitt were born, a war unfolded between two factions: those who supported Suri and those who supported Shiloh. This war changed the landscape of contemporary culture forever.

CECILIA: In 1842, Thomas Scott was born.

*THOMAS SCOTT's portrait comes to life.*

MARIE-ANGELIQUE: In 1844, Louis Riel followed.

*LOUIS RIEL's portrait comes to life.*

With time being what it is—

CECILIA: Cyclical

MARIE-ANGELIQUE: And

EUGENIA: Largely irrelevant

MARIE-ANGELIQUE: And with nothing to prove us wrong, we can only assume a similar war took place between the heroic Monsieur Riel and the villainous Mister Scott.

*A new game begins.*

"In the future, everyone will be famous for fifteen minutes."

CECILIA: Andy Warhol. "Certain shades of limelight wreck a girl's complexion."

MARIE-ANGELIQUE: Truman Capote, *Breakfast at Tiffany's.* "Upon this a question arises: Whether it be better to be loved than feared or feared than loved?"

CECILIA: Niccolò di Bernardo dei Machiavelli!

MARIE-ANGELIQUE: Yes! Ugh hot.

CECILIA: "A hero is no braver than an ordinary man, but he is brave five minutes longer."

MARIE-ANGELIQUE: *(to EUGENIA)* Hey. Are you going to play this time or not?

EUGENIA: I don't like games.

MARIE-ANGELIQUE: Remember what happened last time . . .

EUGENIA: . . . Fine. Ralph Waldo Emerson.

CECILIA: Yay! Fun!

EUGENIA: "I have never in my life yelled at a girl like this. I was rooting for you. We were all rooting for you. How dare you."

MARIE-ANGELIQUE: Tyra Banks, *America's Next Top Model* cycle four.

CECILIA: Penalty. Against the rules.

EUGENIA: Why?

CECILIA: We can't quote women. That doesn't count.

MARIE-ANGELIQUE: She wasn't quoting women; she was quoting Tyra.

CECILIA: Still. It's wrong. You forfeit your turn, and now it's mine. "All who have their reward on earth, the fruits of painful superstition and blind zeal, naught seeking but the praise of men, here find fit retribution, empty as their deed."

MARIE-ANGELIQUE: John Milton, *Paradise Lost*.
I said it first.
Shut up.
You shut up!

EUGENIA: *Paradise Lost*, John Milton.
I said it first.
Shut up.
You shut up!
"Are we human or are we dancer?"

CECILIA: Improper grammar—

EUGENIA: Didn't write it.

Brandon Flowers, heterosexual lead singer of my favourite band, the Killers, and the world's second favourite Mormon after Donny Osmond.

CECILIA: My second favourite Mormon is the man from *Angels in / America*—

MARIE-ANGELIQUE: Nobody asked you who your second favourite Mormon / was—

CECILIA: Nobody ever asks me anything!

> *A baby begins to cry. The portrait of* LOUIS RIEL *intensifies in whatever it's doing. It's a game-changer.*

Is that the tea?

MARIE-ANGELIQUE: "I know that through the grace of God, I am the founder of Manitoba."

EUGENIA: Louis Riel. "Deeds are not accomplished in a few days, or in a few hours. A century is only a spoke in the wheel of everlasting time."

CECILIA: Louis Riel. "We must cherish our inheritance. We must preserve our nationality for the youth of our future. The story should be written down to pass on."

MARIE-ANGELIQUE: Louis Riel. "I am more convinced every day that without a single exception I did right. And I have always believed that, as I have acted honestly, the time will come when the people of Canada will see and acknowledge it."

CECILIA: Louis Riel. "I have nothing but my heart and I have given it long ago to my country."

EUGENIA: Louis Riel. "In a little while it will be over. We may fail. But the rights for which we contend will not die."

MARIE-ANGELIQUE: Louis Riel. "My people will sleep for one hundred years, but when they awake, it will be the artists who give them their spirit back."

*The baby stops crying.*

*The baby was* LOUIS RIEL, *by the way, and he is ready to try again.*

*A new game begins.*

# TWO

**EUGENIA:** The year is—

**MARIE-ANGELIQUE:** Eighteen hundred and something something!

**EUGENIA:** And the place is—

**CECILIA:** A fort!

**EUGENIA:** Somewhere upon the banks of a Reddish River, in—

**ALL:** Treaty One!

> *They say this the way people at a Winnipeg Jets game shout "true north" during the National Anthem.*

**EUGENIA:** —territory, nearish or uponish what is now known as Winnipeg, Manitoba, Canada—

**CECILIA:** Lovely place!

**EUGENIA:** —a city known for simultaneously being the Murder Capital of Canada and the Most Racist City in Canada.

**CECILIA:** We're also the Slurpee Capital of Canada. Don't forget that. That's very important. It should be a part of the treaty, don't you think?

**MARIE-ANGELIQUE:** Honestly, I don't even know what a treaty is.

**CECILIA:** Hard same.

EUGENIA: A treaty is an agreement / between—

CECILIA: We must ask the men! The men will know.

*CECILIA approaches the portrait of THOMAS SCOTT.*

Meet Thomas Scott. Irish. Protestant. Dreamy and delightful. Despite his advanced age of twenty-eight years, he retains many of the assets of his youthful prime, such as silky, smooth, pale alabaster skin that you want to lick as if it's a glazed ham, and luscious long legs that resemble a gazelle. They seem endless, both in terms of length and in terms of possibilities. Although not traditionally handsome, his banging beach bod is so kickin' it makes you forget all about the butterface. And he always parts his light brown hair slightly to the left. I myself am married, but if I wasn't . . .

*CECILIA holds up a doll version of THOMAS SCOTT.*

*(as THOMAS SCOTT)* A treaty is an agreement. And I, for one, would like to honour all of our . . . agreements . . . and humbly acknowledge the traditional lands upon which we stand, and offer a knowledge exchange, a prayer of my people. Treaty, treaty, reconciliation. Treaty, treaty, God bless this nation. Treaty, treaty in a boat, treaty, treaty with a goat. Amen.

*MARIE-ANGELIQUE applauds enthusiastically and gives a standing ovation. EUGENIA applauds patronizingly. She does not give standing ovations, ever.*

MARIE-ANGELIQUE: *Bravo! Fantastique! Très bien! Encore!*

*MARIE-ANGELIQUE runs to the LOUIS RIEL portrait.*

EUGENIA: I beg you, I beg you, please, no more.

MARIE-ANGELIQUE: Louis Riel!!! Métis, like me. Hot, but doesn't even know it. Like, model-level. Despite being hot, he is also smart, which is so rare, y'know? His focus on his work has led him to neglect his appearance, so he's kind of undernourished in that tortured artist way . . . he's a bit dishevelled, and you really have to peer through the layers to see the true beauty within his heart. Also, I think he wears glasses? Because he's a bit of a nerd, which is good! Or else he would be totally unrelatable and intimidating to women. Louis Riel.

*MARIE-ANGELIQUE pulls out a LOUIS RIEL doll. Another game.*

CECILIA: *(as THOMAS SCOTT)* Louis Riel.

MARIE-ANGELIQUE: *(as LOUIS RIEL)* Thomas Scott.

CECILIA: *(as THOMAS SCOTT)* Big Lou.

MARIE-ANGELIQUE: *(as LOUIS RIEL)* Tiny Tom.

CECILIA: *(as THOMAS SCOTT)* How did you find me here?

MARIE-ANGELIQUE: *(as LOUIS RIEL)* Instagram.

CECILIA: *(as THOMAS SCOTT)* I specifically asked them not to tag me.

MARIE-ANGELIQUE: *(as LOUIS RIEL)* It hurts, doesn't it? When you are betrayed by the people you trust the most . . . the people you thought were your friends.

CECILIA: *(as THOMAS SCOTT)* What are you implying?

MARIE-ANGELIQUE: *(as LOUIS RIEL)* I know you've come to steal our land and I refuse to let that happen!

CECILIA: *(as THOMAS SCOTT)* Oh, pish posh. Give it up, old sport. You'll never win, Louis. Or should I call you Lewis?

MARIE-ANGELIQUE: *(as LOUIS RIEL)* Don't, man. You know I hate that.

CECILIA: *(as THOMAS SCOTT)* The land will be ours eventually, whether you half-breeds and savages hand it over to us or we take it by force.

MARIE-ANGELIQUE: *(as LOUIS RIEL)* We will never give this land to you!!!

CECILIA: *(as THOMAS SCOTT)* It is unstoppable. It is manifest destiny.

MARIE-ANGELIQUE: *(as LOUIS RIEL)* Your mom manifested my destiny last night.

CECILIA: *(as THOMAS SCOTT)* Wow. Well. I guess this is it. Guess this is war.

MARIE-ANGELIQUE: *(as LOUIS RIEL)* Looks like it.

CECILIA: *(as THOMAS SCOTT)* I'm unfollowing you.

MARIE-ANGELIQUE: *(as LOUIS RIEL)* Like I care.

CECILIA: *(as THOMAS SCOTT)* I'm leaving.

MARIE-ANGELIQUE: *(as LOUIS RIEL)* No, I'm leaving.

CECILIA: *(as THOMAS SCOTT)* I'm leaving first.

MARIE-ANGELIQUE: *(as LOUIS RIEL)* I'm already gone.

CECILIA: *(as THOMAS SCOTT)* I was never even here.

MARIE-ANGELIQUE: *(as LOUIS RIEL)* I'm an astral projection.

CECILIA: *(as THOMAS SCOTT)* I'm a hologram.

MARIE-ANGELIQUE: *(as LOUIS RIEL)* *Au revoir*, sir.

CECILIA: *(as THOMAS SCOTT)* See you on the battlefield.

MARIE-ANGELIQUE: *(as LOUIS RIEL)* Maybe I'll see you there or maybe I'll see you somewhere else.

CECILIA: . . . Uh, sorry, is he coming to the battlefield or what?

MARIE-ANGELIQUE: Oh yeah yeah, for sure, he'll totally be there.

EUGENIA: Aaaaaanyway.

*MARIE-ANGELIQUE and CECILIA get serious.*

The fort in which we live is a totally normal fort with nothing suspicious happening.

CECILIA: It is a fort much like Lower Fort Garry or Upper Fort Garry, but it is not either of the actual Fort Garrys.

MARIE-ANGELIQUE: It has never even heard of anybody named Garry. And who are we? We are the Women of the Fur Trade. You probably haven't heard of us. That's okay: we probably haven't heard of you either.

*A triangle dings.*

EUGENIA: I must go.

CECILIA: Again?

EUGENIA: Yes, again. Have fun, be safe, don't sit in my chair, and I'll catch you two on the flippity flip.

*EUGENIA boogies off into the night, blowing a kiss to the portrait of Gabriel Dumont on her way out.*

# THREE

*MARIE-ANGELIQUE stands up and sits in EUGENIA's chair: another game begins, one that continues in perpetuity.*

*MARIE-ANGELIQUE and CECILIA rock back and forth and back and forth and back and forth in the rocking chairs, in perfect unison, caressing their dolls.*

**MARIE-ANGELIQUE:** *(about LOUIS RIEL)* I hear he's tall. Taller than me. Six foot three, easy peasy. Like Castro.

**CECILIA:** *(about THOMAS SCOTT)* I hear he's buff. Huge muscles. Benches four hundred, never breaks a sweat.

**MARIE-ANGELIQUE:** He's an inspiring leader. Charismatic. Great at speeches.

**CECILIA:** He's confident and masculine and doesn't need anyone's approval for anything.

**MARIE-ANGELIQUE:** So brave, so courageous, always ready for battle.

**CECILIA:** So smart. So wise. He has seen the world and knows all its secrets.

**MARIE-ANGELIQUE:** Decisive. Definitive.

**CECILIA:** Pious. Devout.

**MARIE-ANGELIQUE:** He never, ever yells.

CECILIA: And he's greatly esteemed by all who encounter him.

MARIE-ANGELIQUE: Truly, a hero.

CECILIA: A hero, truly.

*They swoon like fictional characters in a Harlequin romance novel.*

MARIE-ANGELIQUE: Do you really believe in manifest destiny?

CECILIA: What? No, no, no, no nono, I was simply being . . . Thomas Scott. Presumably he does. My husband sure does.

MARIE-ANGELIQUE: Ew.

CECILIA: I know. But you have nothing to worry about. You fit in here so well, sitting and rocking and smiling.

*MARIE-ANGELIQUE smiles.*

MARIE-ANGELIQUE: I wish I could meet him. He's so hot. I feel such a . . . kinship.

CECILIA: I don't think kinship is the word for that feeling, but okay.

MARIE-ANGELIQUE: I feel like I'm on fire inside.

CECILIA: Yeah, not kinship.

MARIE-ANGELIQUE: Eugenia is so lucky. She gets to leave whenever she wants. She gets to go anywhere and do anything. She could be with Louis Riel right now. They could be having—

CECILIA: Kinship?

MARIE-ANGELIQUE: Do not mock me, Cecilia. There is a reckoning coming and I intend to reckon with it. I believe in Louis Riel and I believe that there is more to life than sitting and rocking and drinking tea. And if I've learned anything useful from my mother at all, which is unlikely, it would be this: if you can believe it, you can achieve it.

CECILIA: How *is* your mother?

MARIE-ANGELIQUE: Let's not ruin a beautiful day by thinking of horrible things.

*CECILIA coughs.*

Are you okay?

CECILIA: A tickle in my throat. Absolutely nothing serious (or relevant to the plot).

MARIE-ANGELIQUE: Mmmmmmkay. Ugh. I'm so bored here. Free me, Louis. I'm your number one fan!

CECILIA: My husband met him once. Did not think very highly of him.

MARIE-ANGELIQUE: Yes, but your husband is friends with John A. Macdonald, prime minister of Canada and the most tiresome and least hot man on the planet.

*MARIE-ANGELIQUE stops rocking in her chair and gasps.*

Ooh. Your husband! PERHAPS. Perhaps you could speak to him on my behalf. Perhaps something could be arranged. A spontaneous, unplanned meeting? An accidental encounter? You are my oldest and dearest and only friend, and I admire you most ardently, and would be loyal to you forever in exchange for this one small favour.

CECILIA: I am happy to try, of course, for you and for our eternal, unbreakable, very stable friendship. But I doubt he'll help. All he cares about is land.

MARIE-ANGELIQUE: This is about the land!

CECILIA: And crops.

MARIE-ANGELIQUE: Crops grow on land!

CECILIA: And sons.

> CECILIA *rubs her stomach. I should have mentioned this before, but she is visibly pregnant.*

It's been girls, girls, girls all up in here.

MARIE-ANGELIQUE: I do hope for your husband's sake that your next baby is a boy. What will you name it?

CECILIA: Victoria, if it is a girl, after the queen, of course. If it's a boy, I was thinking maybe . . . Thomas, after . . . after . . .

> CECILIA *gazes adoringly at her* THOMAS SCOTT.

MARIE-ANGELIQUE: Yikes.

CECILIA: Yeah, I know, but he's just so cute.

MARIE-ANGELIQUE: He's a member of the Canadian Party, and an Orangeman, *and* a Protestant. That's three very not cool things.

CECILIA: I think that depends on who you ask.

MARIE-ANGELIQUE: He wants to take our land and kill us all!

CECILIA: Not *me*, *I'm* white.

MARIE-ANGELIQUE: Sometimes I don't know whose side you're on.

CECILIA: Honestly? Same. But I would never betray you, Marie-Angelique. Pinky swear.

MARIE-ANGELIQUE: . . . Pinky swear. Friends forever. No man, no land, and no government shall ever come between us. We'll always have each other's backs.

*They pinky swear.*

# FOUR

*EUGENIA re-enters with a handbag full of furs.*

**EUGENIA:** Yo. Got furs.

**CECILIA:** Eugenia!

**MARIE-ANGELIQUE:** What are you doing back so soon?

**EUGENIA:** The seasons have been shorter lately. And I'm very efficient. Why are you in my chair? I told you not to sit in my chair.

*MARIE-ANGELIQUE stands up and moves back to her original rocking chair. EUGENIA sits down in her rightful traditional spot.*

**CECILIA:** Welcome back, my dear friend.

**MARIE-ANGELIQUE:** Any news? Will there be a rebellion? I've always wanted to be part of a rebellion.

*The sound of a boiling teapot.*

**EUGENIA:** It is imminent.

**MARIE-ANGELIQUE:** I knew it! I knew Confederation was a dumb-ass idea.

**CECILIA:** Hopefully the battle will not reach us. I will pray for peace and our safety. Our Father, who art in—

*The tea is ready.*

Oh! The tea is ready. It's time for tea! Shall we have some tea? Tee hee.

*CECILIA gives each of the women a teacup, a saucer, and a spoon.*

**MARIE-ANGELIQUE:** *Merci.*

**CECILIA:** *La bibliothèque.*

**EUGENIA:** *Miigwetch.*

**CECILIA:** Oooh and a very May-witch to you to!

*The three women raise their teacups and have a silent toast. MARIE-ANGELIQUE and CECILIA each take a sip. It's apparently delish.*

Yum.

*EUGENIA turns her teacup over. Nothing drips out.*

**EUGENIA:** There's nothing in this / cup—

**CECILIA:** Eugenia, where do you go when you leave us behind?

**EUGENIA:** All over. Wherever I want.

**CECILIA:** Isn't it dangerous?

**EUGENIA:** Of course. But it's dangerous here too.

*EUGENIA motions to the men.*

**MARIE-ANGELIQUE:** I kind of like them. I like being watched.

EUGENIA: I bet they'd love to watch you even more if you were wearing, say, a new fur hat?

*EUGENIA pulls out a fur hat.*

MARIE-ANGELIQUE: Oh, it's beautiful! But I have nothing to trade! And I have none of that new-fangled Confederate currency because I don't have a new-fangled Confederate husband. God, my life sucks.

EUGENIA: Cecilia?

CECILIA: My husband will no longer trade with women. He says it's against the Lord's will. Says it is not natural for women to be off in the world, working alongside men.

EUGENIA: Weird. Where I come from, women were always responsible for trading. You can't trust men with important jobs. Best just send them off to like fishing or a war, somewhere they won't be in the way, and bring them back when you need them, if you know what I mean. But, quite frankly, in my opinion, there's almost nothing a man can do that a woman can't do . . . including that, again, if you know what I mean. And I know you do, Cecilia.

CECILIA: I most certainly do not!

MARIE-ANGELIQUE: What do you mean?

CECILIA: You'll find out when you're married.

MARIE-ANGELIQUE: Do you mean intercourse?

CECILIA: It is not appropriate for women to speak of such things.

EUGENIA: Where I'm from, women always—

CECILIA: We are no longer where you're from. That world is gone.

EUGENIA: A final gasp. A dying breath. A good fur trade.

MARIE-ANGELIQUE: It is not dead yet. Our way of life can still be saved. And we can all still be friends and trade furs forever! Fur-ever! Haha! Trust me. Louis Riel will see to it.

EUGENIA: Ugh.

MARIE-ANGELIQUE: May I help you?

EUGENIA: Everywhere I go that's all I hear. Louis Riel this, Louis Riel that. He's overrated.

MARIE-ANGELIQUE: Blasphemer.

CECILIA: I've heard he is very pious and devout, although there are murmurs that he may be a . . . whisper voice traitor end whisper voice.

MARIE-ANGELIQUE: Even a traitor deserves forgiveness.

EUGENIA: His face looks like a potato.

MARIE-ANGELIQUE: Potatoes are delicious. I'm sure Thomas Scott would agree.

CECILIA: Very rude.

EUGENIA: And what's with his facial hair? A mustache with no beard?

MARIE-ANGELIQUE: He's a trendsetter.

CECILIA: Your mother would never approve.

MARIE-ANGELIQUE: My mother is a selfish, miserable hag and I'll never forgive her.

EUGENIA: Didn't you just say that "even a traitor deserves forgiveness"?

MARIE-ANGELIQUE: We digress from the important matter at hand: the newly formed country of Canada is intent on destroying our way of life and I must use all of my skills and all of my gumption to survive! I am like the Scarlett O'Hara of the prairies, and I will do whatever it takes to protect my people. And I will also go on record to say that it has always been childhood dream to marry a Métis man and keep our culture alive.

CECILIA: No, it wasn't. You've always loved basic white boys.

MARIE-ANGELIQUE: They're just so confident, for no good reason!

EUGENIA: Do we even know for sure if he is Métis? He could be faking it. People do that all the time, for book deals.

CECILIA: I believe he is Ojibwe, Eugenia. Like you.

EUGENIA: He's *Franco*-Ojibwe. That's completely different.

CECILIA: How is it different?

EUGENIA: Well, for one, I don't *parle pas français*.

MARIE-ANGELIQUE: You do too *parle pas français*. We all *parle pas français*.

EUGENIA: Mine's *no bueno*.

MARIE-ANGELIQUE: It is no longer fashionable to look down upon the French, Eugenia. It is *très* chic now. The Russians, for instance, can't get enough of it.

CECILIA: TOLSTOY.

MARIE-ANGELIQUE: Exactly.

EUGENIA: But why marriage? That's not fun.

CECILIA: I'm having a great time.

MARIE-ANGELIQUE: Because I'm not like you, Eugenia. I can't just leave here whenever I want. I can't trap or hunt or take care of myself. If I get married, I'll be protected . . . and maybe then I can protect others. Louis Riel is surely at the forefront of the fight for our rights, and that fight will inevitably bring him here. And when it does, I'll be ready.

EUGENIA: Even if you did someday meet him, there's no telling you'd like him.

MARIE-ANGELIQUE: That's okay. You don't have to like someone to marry them. You just have to love them.

EUGENIA: I don't intend to ever get married. I like being free.

MARIE-ANGELIQUE: I can be free and be a wife at the same time.

CECILIA: No. You must submit to your husband fully. Every decision he makes, you must support.

MARIE-ANGELIQUE: I'll simply pray he makes good choices.

EUGENIA: Last I heard, he had dropped out of school and was living in Chicago writing, like, poetry.

MARIE-ANGELIQUE: Can you please just be happy for me? I finally have a purpose.

EUGENIA: You have a crush.

**MARIE-ANGELIQUE:** I have a goal.

**EUGENIA:** A lofty one. You've never left this room.

**MARIE-ANGELIQUE:** He'll find me.

**EUGENIA:** It's not an easy door to find. And he is likely still very far away.

**MARIE-ANGELIQUE:** Distance is no barrier. Love knows no obstacles. And "as long as we have love, love will keep us together."

*A letter magically drops from the ceiling and onto* CECILIA's *lap. She picks it up and reads it.*

**CECILIA:** Prithee, hark. I have just received a letter from my husband. He will be returning to Red River shortly, alongside his expedition, on the trail of a certain . . . Marie-Angelique, you will find this news of particular interest . . . Mister Louis Riel.

**MARIE-ANGELIQUE:** Oh my god.

**EUGENIA:** The trail of who?

**MARIE-ANGELIQUE:** Oh my god.

**CECILIA:** Louis Riel.

*EUGENIA begins rocking in her chair. She rocks back and forth and back and forth and back and forth.*

**MARIE-ANGELIQUE:** Oh my god, it's all happening. This is happening. This is really happening. I honestly thought I was being a little unreasonable, but this is . . . all my dreams are coming true! Everything I've worked so hard for! Every croissant I never ate, every Pilates class I ever attended, every time I told my former crush, Matthew the

Incompetent Blacksmith, "No, I'm saving myself for Louis Riel"—it was all worth it. Because I was. I truly was.

EUGENIA: Matthew the Incompetent Blacksmith is a good, kind man. He's a wise match and he looks great shirtless and can make dope swords.

MARIE-ANGELIQUE: But I love another!

EUGENIA: No, you don't. You've never even met him.

MARIE-ANGELIQUE: So what? None of us have.

*EUGENIA stops rocking.*

EUGENIA: Eh. Well.

| MARIE-ANGELIQUE: No. | CECILIA: No way. |
|---|---|
| Wait what? | Huh? |
| Have you? | You have? |
| Oh my god. | Oh, my lanta. |
| You've met Louis Riel? | You've met Louis Riel! |

*MARIE-ANGELIQUE and CECILIA shriek with excitement and maybe a little bit of jealousy.*

MARIE-ANGELIQUE: My future husband is coming home and my dearest, bestest, and onlyest friend will introduce us!

*MARIE-ANGELIQUE warmly embraces EUGENIA. CECILIA gasps.*

EUGENIA: I always got the feeling you didn't like me very much.

MARIE-ANGELIQUE: Nonsense! You are my best friend forever—

CECILIA: Hey, what about ME?

**MARIE-ANGELIQUE:** —and *you* will introduce me to Louis Riel!

**CECILIA:** I thought I was your best friend.

**MARIE-ANGELIQUE:** Best friend is a tier, not a person.

**EUGENIA:** He's so . . . mediocre.

**MARIE-ANGELIQUE:** He is not mediocre. He is . . . he's . . . he's a man. He matters.

**CECILIA:** How well *do* you know him, Eugenia?

**EUGENIA:** Surely it would be improper to discuss such things.

**MARIE-ANGELIQUE:** Liar.

**CECILIA:** Scandalous.

**MARIE-ANGELIQUE:** He would never. He's too good for you.

*Beat.*

You will introduce me, won't you?

**EUGENIA:** I don't know if that's a good idea.

**MARIE-ANGELIQUE:** I'll buy a hat.

**EUGENIA:** With what? You don't have any money.

*MARIE-ANGELIQUE takes off her necklace.*

**MARIE-ANGELIQUE:** Here. A trade. It was my mother's, she made it herself.

EUGENIA: It's too valuable.

MARIE-ANGELIQUE: Take it. If you don't sell these hats your family will starve, won't they? So take it. It's valuable. And it doesn't mean anything to me anymore.

*They trade.*

CECILIA: Oh, Marie-Angelique, your lifelong dream is about to come true.

MARIE-ANGELIQUE: Yes, it is. For soon I shall be on my way to becoming Mrs. Louis Riel!

*And with a grand flourish, she puts on her fluffy new hat.*

# FIVE

*The women each grab a piece of paper and a quill—but no ink— from their bags, and each begin to compose a letter.*

CECILIA: Dear Husband,

EUGENIA: Dear Prime Minister,

MARIE-ANGELIQUE: Dear Louis,

EUGENIA: How dare you.

CECILIA: Your child was born, a sweet little girl.

MARIE-ANGELIQUE: You don't know me, and we've never met, but I am writing to you now to profess my undying love.

EUGENIA: I hate you.

CECILIA: Curly, blond hair with fair skin.

MARIE-ANGELIQUE: Forgive me if that's forward, but I am a very direct person and I am confident you will find my assertiveness charming, for you have such wonderful taste in all areas of your life.

EUGENIA: It's time to make way, for the times are changing.

CECILIA: Very Aryan.

MARIE-ANGELIQUE: I would like to be so bold as to propose a meeting between the two of us, upon your return to the Reddish River.

CECILIA: I miss you.

EUGENIA: Our turtle's back has been burdened by your boringness for far too long.

CECILIA: I can't live without you by my side.

MARIE-ANGELIQUE: Our mutual friend, dear sweet Eugenia, believes we will get along swimmingly, and I agree.

CECILIA: You are so honourable to fight for our safety, but I really think a job closer to home would be best for our growing family.

EUGENIA: You need to watch how a real leader leads and change your plans.

MARIE-ANGELIQUE: Oh yes, my name is Marie-Angelique.

CECILIA: Your children love you and so do I.

EUGENIA: The world is rearranging, it's marching onward, and time moves on without those who refuse to evolve.

CECILIA: We pray for your safe return every night.

MARIE-ANGELIQUE: I am twenty-two years old, and a Taurus with Sun rising in Leo, so I hate change, and as you are a Libra on the cusp of Scorpio, I envision a thrilling meeting of the minds is fated for us.

CECILIA: And Thomas Scott too, I hope that he's all right.

EUGENIA: Revolution is in the air.

MARIE-ANGELIQUE: I eagerly await your arrival to our beautiful fort. I can't wait to meet you and hope I may be able to contribute meaningfully to your noble cause.

EUGENIA: You'll be lost and left behind, and I will celebrate with Prosecco and strawberries.

CECILIA: He is a lovely man, with an excellent side part, and is an asset to our chance for survival.

MARIE-ANGELIQUE: Some people may call you selfish, but I value your devoted leadership.

EUGENIA: "You may take our land, you may take our lives, but you will never take our freedom."

CECILIA: I hope we can withstand the transformation.

EUGENIA: Mel Gibson, *Braveheart*.

MARIE-ANGELIQUE: You are a Métis man of esteem and prestige.

CECILIA: I must admit I have some hesitation.

MARIE-ANGELIQUE: And I am a Métis woman of . . . well, let's just say, you could do worse.

EUGENIA: If you hurt Gabriel Dumont, I will end you.

CECILIA: But I pray each day for a better nation.

MARIE-ANGELIQUE: Goodbye for now, and safe travels.

CECILIA: Your obedient wife,

EUGENIA: Fuck off and die,

MARIE-ANGELIQUE: Lots of love,

CECILIA: Cecilia.

EUGENIA: Your mom.

MARIE-ANGELIQUE: Marie-Angelique! Xoxo.

*EUGENIA and MARIE-ANGELIQUE seal up their letters.*

CECILIA: P.S. Do hurry back. The conflict marches ever closer, and I fear for my safety and the safety of our children.

*CECILIA seals up her letter. She has a slight coughing fit. The three women throw their letters high in the air, where they are picked up by Canada Post and delivered in a timely and efficient manner.*

# SIX

*Meanwhile, deep inside the portraits and far beyond the walls of the Not-Fort-Garry Fort Garry sit* THOMAS SCOTT *and* LOUIS RIEL *in two non-rocking chairs. They do not wear furs. They do not drink tea. They do not look anything like their portraits.*

*LOUIS dictates the end of a letter to* THOMAS.

**LOUIS RIEL:** . . . and in conclusion, mark my words, the prairies will be alive once more with the sound of music, the sound of drums, the sound of war. The sanguine fluid of our enemies, our friends, and ourselves will circumvolute and transmogrify the waters of the Reddish River and turn it into a river of blood and a tributary of forsaken dreams. Have a great day, your friend, Louis Riel.

**THOMAS SCOTT:** That's nice. Very poetic.

**LOUIS RIEL:** It's not nice.

**THOMAS SCOTT:** Okay.

**LOUIS RIEL:** Nice is a cowardly word, Thomas.

**THOMAS SCOTT:** Okay.

**LOUIS RIEL:** Do better next time.

**THOMAS SCOTT:** Okay.

*THOMAS finishes the letter and throws it up for express delivery.*

Done.

*LOUIS is silent.*

You're welcome.

**LOUIS RIEL:** Hm? Oh. Thanks, man.

*THOMAS smiles. He's a little starved for gratitude. His confidence has risen enormously.*

**THOMAS SCOTT:** You're welcome, Louis.

*Beat.*

Hey, man?

**LOUIS RIEL:** Yeah, man?

**THOMAS SCOTT:** Can we talk? Like man to man?

**LOUIS RIEL:** Bro to bro?

**THOMAS SCOTT:** Yeah.

**LOUIS RIEL:** Cool dude to cool dude.

**THOMAS SCOTT:** Okay sure.

**LOUIS RIEL:** Then okay sure to you too also as well.

**THOMAS SCOTT:** Right. Um, so I love, first of all, writing all your letters for you. I really do. I'm honoured. It's just the best how you get so many letters and I don't get any, so it's great, it's . . . so good . . . just . . . writing things . . . for you, and not for me, but uh . . . like I'm glad my hands are keeping busy or else, you know, who knows what else I'd be doing with them, haha that was a joke, you didn't get it, sorry. Look, Louis, I know we've had our differences, but . . . sorry, I don't know exactly how to say this, I—

LOUIS RIEL: Say it like a man, Thomas.

THOMAS SCOTT: I . . . okay. *(deeper voice)* I sometimes feel like, like, like, like you—

LOUIS RIEL: A real man never stutters.

THOMAS SCOTT: Sorry.

LOUIS RIEL: Start again. Use your words.

> *THOMAS clears his throat.*

THOMAS SCOTT: Sometimes. I feel. Like you. Don't respect. Me.

LOUIS RIEL: And?

THOMAS SCOTT: That was it. That's all.

LOUIS RIEL: Hm.

THOMAS SCOTT: Well, do-do you?

LOUIS RIEL: Do I what?

THOMAS SCOTT: Respect me?

LOUIS RIEL: Does the grey wolf respect the Connemara pony?

THOMAS SCOTT: I beg your pardon.

LOUIS RIEL: You heard me.

THOMAS SCOTT: I heard you, but I didn't hear you. I'm going to need additional context.

LOUIS RIEL: I'm a grey wolf, a highly revered and feared animal here on the prairies, and you are a mere Irish pony, the natural prey of wolves like me. See, you're not even a horse, Thomas, you're a pony.

That's a tiny horse.

THOMAS SCOTT: I know what a pony is.

LOUIS RIEL: Good.

THOMAS SCOTT: But you should know that wolves went extinct in Ireland over a hundred years ago.

LOUIS RIEL: You're not in Ireland anymore, old sport. This is Canada: a much more dangerous place, for all of us; wolves and ponies alike.

*Suddenly, a letter falls from the sky and into LOUIS's lap. He inspects it. It has a bright lipstick mark on it.*

Ugh, not another one.

*LOUIS fans himself lackadaisically.*

THOMAS SCOTT: Ooh! Are you going to read it?

LOUIS RIEL: There's a war going on, Thomas. I don't have time for love letters.

THOMAS SCOTT: I wish I'd get a love letter.

LOUIS RIEL: Then why don't you read it?

THOMAS SCOTT: Really?

**LOUIS RIEL:** Sure. Knock yourself out.

*LOUIS hands THOMAS the letter. THOMAS opens it and begins to read.*

**THOMAS SCOTT:** "Dear Louis,

You don't know me, and we've never met, but I am writing to you now to profess my undying love." Wow. That's bold.

**LOUIS RIEL:** I meant read it silently to yourself.

**THOMAS SCOTT:** Okay, sorry.

**LOUIS RIEL:** Well now I'm invested, so keep reading aloud.

**THOMAS SCOTT:** Okay. "I would like to be so bold—" BOLD "—as to propose a meeting between the two of us, upon your return to the Reddish River." Reddish River? I thought we were going to Gettysburg.

**LOUIS RIEL:** What made you think that?

**THOMAS SCOTT:** Three days ago, you said, "Thomas, do you want to go to Gettysburg with me?" And I said, "Why are you asking me? Don't you hate me?" And then you said—

**LOUIS RIEL:** I remember what I said.

**THOMAS SCOTT:** What's in Reddish River? Why are we going there and not to Gettysburg, the site of the greatest battle of the Civil War?

**LOUIS RIEL:** Do you want to visit the site where history was made, or do you want to be the one to make history?

**THOMAS SCOTT:** I don't know. I just want to be happy. What do you want to do?

**LOUIS RIEL:** Everyone expects me to go to Reddish River. They expect me to fight. But that's not me, is it? I'm just a simple poet with a great moustache. I yearn for love, not for war. I want to be held and caressed and—

**THOMAS SCOTT:** Okay. "Our mutual friend, dear sweet Eugenia, believes we will get along swimmingly, and I agree. Oh yes, my name is Marie-Angelique. I am—"

**LOUIS RIEL:** What did you say?

**THOMAS SCOTT:** What?

**LOUIS RIEL:** What was that name again?

**THOMAS SCOTT:** Marie-Angelique? Beautiful name.

**LOUIS RIEL:** Before that.

**THOMAS SCOTT:** Oh, Eugenia? That's good too.

**LOUIS RIEL:** Eugenia.

**THOMAS SCOTT:** That's right, Eugenia. Like Eugene but with an ia.

**LOUIS RIEL:** Eugenia. Temptress. Seductress. Siren.

**THOMAS SCOTT:** Ooh, it sounds like there's a story here.

**LOUIS RIEL:** Shut up, Thomas.

**THOMAS SCOTT:** Sounds like we'll hear the story later.

**LOUIS RIEL:** She's in Reddish River, you say?

**THOMAS SCOTT:** Well, Marie-Angelique says. I'm just reading.

**LOUIS RIEL:** Hm. Well. Continue.

**THOMAS SCOTT:** "I am twenty-two years old, and a Taurus with Sun rising in Leo, so I hate change." Hey, that's interesting, I hate change too!

**LOUIS RIEL:** Change is the only thing we can count on. Change is a harbinger of . . . more change.

**THOMAS SCOTT:** " . . . and as you are a Libra on the cusp of Scorpio, I envision a thrilling meeting of the minds is fated for us."

**LOUIS RIEL:** Hm. I don't believe in astrology . . . but I do believe in fate.

**THOMAS SCOTT:** "I eagerly await your arrival to our beautiful fort. I can't wait to meet you and hope I may be able to contribute meaningfully to your noble cause."

**LOUIS RIEL:** Is this a sign? Is this my destiny?

**THOMAS SCOTT:** "Some people may call you selfish," ow, harsh but true, "but I value your devoted leadership."

**LOUIS RIEL:** Can I be both a great poet and a great leader?

**THOMAS SCOTT:** "You are a Métis man of esteem and prestige. And I am a Métis woman of . . . well, let's just say, you could do worse." You hear that? You could do worse!

**LOUIS RIEL:** She could do worse. I've got poems to write . . . and a war to win.

**THOMAS SCOTT:** "Goodbye for now, and safe travels. Lots of love, Marie-Angelique! Xoxo." Aw. That's how I sign my letters too.

*THOMAS preps a piece of paper, ready to respond.*

I'm ready. What is your response?

LOUIS RIEL: I don't have time for a response. I have a war to win.

THOMAS SCOTT: You said that already.

LOUIS RIEL: Did I? Or did you just hear me twice?

THOMAS SCOTT: Uh both?

LOUIS RIEL: Hm. Right. *Right.*

> LOUIS *stands and prepares to leave.*

THOMAS SCOTT: Where are you going?

LOUIS RIEL: Reddish River.

THOMAS SCOTT: But Gettysburg—

LOUIS RIEL: Gettysburg can wait.

THOMAS SCOTT: Is this about that woman?

LOUIS RIEL: This is about destiny. I'm leaving at dawn.

THOMAS SCOTT: Do you want me to join you?

LOUIS RIEL: Join me, or don't.

THOMAS SCOTT: Okay, I will.

LOUIS RIEL: Great.

> LOUIS *leaves to pack his Louis Vuitton suitcase.*

**THOMAS SCOTT:** Reddish River. Could be fun. Could be a life out there for me. Could be land out there for me.

> *THOMAS rereads MARIE-ANGELIQUE's letter, silently.*

And maybe Louis is right. Maybe fate is real. And maybe . . . maybe she could do worse. A lot worse. Maybe she could love . . . me.

> *And he begins to write a love letter of his own.*

# SEVEN

*Back in the fort. The women are still rocking.*

CECILIA: I thought it was a delightful film. After all, I love *Cats* the musical and the animal, but the proportions seemed all askew, didn't you think—

*A letter drops into CECILIA's lap.*

Oh! At last. News from my husband. I'm married, you see.

*CECILIA casually pointedly strokes her wedding ring.*

MARIE-ANGELIQUE: What's the tea?

CECILIA: He writes that William McDougall's arrival is imminent.

EUGENIA: Now there is a handsome man. No moustache. Strong fighter.

MARIE-ANGELIQUE: Where did he fight?

CECILIA: Why, Gettysburg of course.

MARIE-ANGELIQUE: Gettysburg! The bloodiest battle of the Civil War! I've always wanted to visit.

EUGENIA: It would be awful if what happened there happened here.

MARIE-ANGELIQUE: Louis Riel would never let that happen. Our land will be kept healthy and safe. The water will always be fresh, and the trees will grow tall and strong, and all the animals will come back someday. We will build a new world and in this new world all the men will want to trade with you, and you will be rich, and you can bring your family down here to Reddish River!

EUGENIA: I think they like it up north, away from this European garbage fire.

MARIE-ANGELIQUE: Fires spread.

EUGENIA: Yeah. They do.

MARIE-ANGELIQUE: Louis Riel and I . . . we didn't start the fire. It was always burning since the world's been turning, but we will endeavour until our dying day to put that fire out. If the settlers cannot live peacefully upon this land, then they should not live here at all.

CECILIA: I beg your pardon?

MARIE-ANGELIQUE: You heard me.

CECILIA: I haven't done anything wrong. It's not my fault my husband is a—well, quite frankly, I don't know what he does. I just know he's not particularly good at it. But don't put his sins on my shoulders. I thought we were friends forever. We pinky swore.

MARIE-ANGELIQUE: You're right. Sorry for being such a little bitch. The uncertainty of all of this—our room, our fort, our river, our land—is really taking a toll.

CECILIA: I accept your apology, Marie-Angelique. These are trying times. We must stick together and put our belief in the Lord our God.

*CECILIA looks to the heavens and makes the sign of the cross. MARIE-ANGELIQUE copies her, with mild apprehension. EUGENIA follows suit, but does it purposefully wrongly, like Tom Hanks in* A League of Their Own.

MARIE-ANGELIQUE: And in these times uncertain, I endeavour to emerge as a figure of worth and esteem. But I also know that I must have a man beside me to be taken seriously. And who better than Louis Riel. Let us plan the wedding.

CECILIA: Yes, let's. Women grow by men.

EUGENIA: I grow independent and alone.

MARIE-ANGELIQUE: And I grow tall and proud using men to further my purpose. Is that so wrong?

CECILIA: Yes, very.                    EUGENIA: It's a little manipulative
                                       but I'm honestly fine with it.

*A letter drops from the sky into the lap of MARIE-ANGELIQUE. MARIE-ANGELIQUE gasps.*

MARIE-ANGELIQUE: Oh my god. Oh my god. Oh my god oh my god oh my god oh my god oh my GOD oh my god my god oh my oh my oh me oh my my god my dog my word he wrote back! He wrote me! He wrote me a letter! Louis Riel! Wrote me a letter! Louis! Riel! Rebel! Poet! Leader! Hero! Prophet! Moustache!

EUGENIA: You gonna read it or just keep saying words?

MARIE-ANGELIQUE: A letter from Reddish River's very own Che Guevara? Of course I'm going to read it.

*MARIE-ANGELIQUE holds the letter for a while.*

Okay, I can't, I'm too nervous! Cecilia, you do it! Do it in his voice!

CECILIA: I don't know what he sounds like.

MARIE-ANGELIQUE: Try!

*CECILIA grabs the letter, the LOUIS RIEL doll, and clears her throat.*

CECILIA: *(as LOUIS RIEL)* Dear Marie-Angelique,

MARIE-ANGELIQUE: Did you hear that? He called me DEAR!

CECILIA: *(as LOUIS RIEL)* Thank you so much for your warm, inspiring letter. Your observations and insights about me were / most astute.

EUGENIA: Oh my god. You're doing it wrong. He doesn't sound like that at all. Here, give it to me.

*EUGENIA grabs the letter and the doll and takes a stab. It's*
*. . . better, but I don't know if Louis himself would call it accurate.*

*(as LOUIS RIEL)* I have never felt so wholly understood and loved for myself and not for my poetry or my moustache. It seems we have an enormous amount in common, two lost souls swimming in the same colonizer fishbowl, Roman calendar year after Roman calendar year.

EUGENIA & LOUIS RIEL: *(both as LOUIS RIEL)* Your letter came at the perfect time—just as I intend to do—to the fort I mean, not to, well, never mind—because although war is inevitable—

LOUIS RIEL & THOMAS SCOTT: *(as LOUIS RIEL and THOMAS SCOTT)* —with the stimulating support from a beautiful, powerful, Taurean with Leo ascending Métis woman such as yourself engorging my body with the white-hot heat of passion, I am confident that I can remain—

**THOMAS SCOTT:** *(as THOMAS SCOTT)*—erect in the face of the trials before me and protect our world from those who wish to do us harm. Upon my return to Reddish River, it would be my deepest pleasure to meet with you and see if this pulsating connection I sense between us in these letters is as real as I hope it is.

**LOUIS RIEL & THOMAS SCOTT:** *(as LOUIS RIEL and THOMAS SCOTT)* There is so much work to be done, Marie-Angelique.

**EUGENIA & LOUIS RIEL:** *(both as LOUIS RIEL)* And I have felt ever so alone.

**EUGENIA & CECILIA:** *(both as LOUIS RIEL)* Until now. Suddenly the world is filled with wonder and with hope.

**CECILIA:** *(as LOUIS RIEL)* Because suddenly the world is filled with you. Throbbingly yours,

*(as CECILIA)* Louis Riel. Xoxo.

**MARIE-ANGELIQUE:** Holy shit, what the fuck.

**CECILIA:** What a kind letter. He sounds lovely.

**EUGENIA:** Throbbingly? Pulsating? Erect? This doesn't sound like him at all. This doesn't even look like his handwriting.

**MARIE-ANGELIQUE:** Eugenia, important people don't write their own letters. They have less important people do that for them.

**CECILIA:** What will your response be?

**MARIE-ANGELIQUE:** "Yes! Yes, yes, yes. Yes, to all of this. Yes." Oh. Eugenia, hand me my paper and my quill.

EUGENIA: Why? It's closer to you than it is to me. Just get it yourself, it's like right there.

*MARIE-ANGELIQUE begrudgingly picks up her own quill and paper.*

MARIE-ANGELIQUE: Cecilia. Your penmanship is so much more distinguished than mine. Would you do me the honour of being my personal letter writer in my correspondences with Louis Riel?

CECILIA: Yes, of course. It would be my pleasure.

*CECILIA prepares the quill for some hardcore letter-writing.*

MARIE-ANGELIQUE: "Dear Louis Riel,

*Bonjour.* My heart is bursting with joy from your beautiful letter. I am utterly delighted for our upcoming meeting. I will wait patiently here in the fort for your return." Should I give him directions to find me or . . . ?

EUGENIA: No, don't give him any additional information. Let him seek you out. Men love that.

MARIE-ANGELIQUE: So wise. "I have heard tell that a rebellion is imminent, and I endeavour to support you. Don't ask me how, but I have access to many weapons. I am not like other girls, Louis. I am ready to fight. I must fight. It is my duty. This country needs a change, and I think you and I could be that change. Prime Minister John A. Macdonald—"

CECILIA: What does the A stand for?

EUGENIA: Asshole.

MARIE-ANGELIQUE: "—is a most terrible man. I can help you, Louis. I can help you help our people. I see the real you, Louis, and I find it beautiful. Respectfully yours, Marie-Angelique. Xoxo."

*MARIE-ANGELIQUE waits for CECILIA to finish writing the letter.*

Hurry up, hurry up. Why is it taking you so long?

CECILIA: It's the 1800s, everything takes long. I'm writing with a quill.

*Beat.*

. . . May I say something?

MARIE-ANGELIQUE: If you must.

CECILIA: Perhaps it would behoove you to be a touch more demure in your letter? What you're saying here could be misconstrued as treason.

MARIE-ANGELIQUE: It wouldn't be misconstrued. It is treason. I'm committing treason! Wow. Like Marie Antoinette. Mm, I love cake.

EUGENIA: She was guillotined.

MARIE-ANGELIQUE: Ugh hot.

EUGENIA: What?

*CECILIA proudly holds up the letter.*

CECILIA: Finished!

*MARIE-ANGELIQUE seals it with a kiss.*

MARIE-ANGELIQUE: Now we must ensure this letter is sent to the appropriate hands.

*MARIE-ANGELIQUE is about to fling the letter high in the air, but EUGENIA stops her.*

EUGENIA: No! If this letter gets into the wrong hands . . . you cannot place your trust in Canada Post. If you are formally going to align yourself with Louis Riel, you must be more careful now. There are enemies everywhere.

*CECILIA grabs the letter.*

CECILIA: My husband can take it and bring it east to the—

*MARIE-ANGELIQUE slaps CECILIA's hand. CECILIA drops the letter.*

MARIE-ANGELIQUE: No!

EUGENIA: No!

CECILIA: Great jumping Jehoshaphat.

MARIE-ANGELIQUE: Who is Jehoshaphat?

CECILIA: The fourth king of Judah.

MARIE-ANGELIQUE: Why do you know that? You're not Jewish. This is the fur trade; nobody here is Jewish!

CECILIA: Surely some people here are Jewish. Besides, I trust my husband with my life.

EUGENIA: Yes, but do you trust him with ours? Your husband hates Louis Riel.

CECILIA: He doesn't hate Louis Riel! He just doesn't know Louis Riel. And he just thinks that Louis Riel is a dangerous force in the imperial quest to colonize Canada and free it from the shackles of the Indians.

MARIE-ANGELIQUE: Excuse me, Native Americans.

EUGENIA: Aboriginals.

MARIE-ANGELIQUE: First Nations . . . ?

EUGENIA: . . . Indigenous?

MARIE-ANGELIQUE: Ya that's good I can get on board with that.

EUGENIA: No offence, Cecilia, but your husband is a bit of a tool. How do you not punch him like every day?

CECILIA: In my defence, I very rarely see him. And I don't agree with him, necessarily.

*Beat.*

And even if I did, you are still my dearest friends.

*Beat.*

Couldn't we not simply agree to disagree?

*Beets.*

He does strive for your safety, Marie-Angelique, and the safety of all the Métis and the Indian . . . Native . . . First Nations Aboriginal Indigenous peoples.

*A triangle dings.*

EUGENIA: It's that time again. Here. Give me the letter. I'll do it.

MARIE-ANGELIQUE: You will?

CECILIA: But it's so dangerous out there.

EUGENIA: This is Canada. It's dangerous everywhere.

MARIE-ANGELIQUE: *Miigwetch.*

EUGENIA: See you again soon.

> *Letter in hand,* EUGENIA *peaces the heck out.* MARIE-ANGELIQUE
> *and* CECILIA *sit quietly in their rocking chairs.*

MARIE-ANGELIQUE: How come she gets to leave all the time and I can't even find the door?

CECILIA: There's a door?

MARIE-ANGELIQUE: There must be. How else did I get here? How else does she come and go so easily?

CECILIA: I've never thought about it before. I like sitting here. Although it would be interesting, wouldn't it? Walking through a door.

MARIE-ANGELIQUE: I must have walked through a door before. I don't remember it. I wish I could.

CECILIA: I'm sure you'll walk through a door again someday, Marie-Angelique, if it is what you truly want.

MARIE-ANGELIQUE: . . . I think . . . I think it is.

CECILIA: I bet Louis Riel walks through doors all the time.

MARIE-ANGELIQUE: Yeah. *Yeah.* And soon, I will join him.

CECILIA: Yeah. *Yeah.* Well, the letter is written and on its way to its destination. And now it is time for us to perform our womanly duties and sit quietly. Oh, isn't life grand upon the banks of the Reddish River? Nothing bad could ever happen to us here.

*The women sip their tea. EUGENIA re-enters.*

EUGENIA: That's weird.

CECILIA: Back so soon?

MARIE-ANGELIQUE: How long have we been drinking tea?

EUGENIA: No . . . I didn't leave.

CECILIA: Why not?

EUGENIA: I can't find the door. It's gone.

> *EUGENIA sits back in her chair. She rocks back and forth and back and forth and back and forth, faster and faster and faster until coming to a complete stop.*

CECILIA: Hmm. Well. S'more tea?

> *CECILIA gives MARIE-ANGELIQUE and EUGENIA some more tea. CECILIA takes a sip of hers. She coughs.*

# EIGHT

*Back with the boys, en route to the Reddish River, setting up camp for the evening.*

THOMAS SCOTT: How much longer?

LOUIS RIEL: Not long.

THOMAS SCOTT: Right. I'm nervous.

LOUIS RIEL: You should be. You won't be greeted warmly.

THOMAS SCOTT: But we've been exchanging the loveliest letters.

LOUIS RIEL: Who?

THOMAS SCOTT: Me and the girl. Marie-Angelique. You told me to write her back, so I did.

LOUIS RIEL: I didn't tell you to do that.

THOMAS SCOTT: Yeah you did. You said, "She could do worse." And the only thing worse than you is . . . me.

LOUIS RIEL: That's a really sad way to think of yourself. Also, not a particularly pleasant way to describe me.

THOMAS SCOTT: Well we've all got problems, Louis. The world doesn't just revolve around you, you know. I'm a person, not a punching bag.

Has it ever occurred to you that I'm actually the one with more power here? I'm white.

LOUIS RIEL: What? I didn't notice.

THOMAS SCOTT: The government isn't the enemy, Louis. You said yourself that you love change—this is change. This is the future. Fighting against change is . . . it's selfish.

LOUIS RIEL: That land belongs to itself, not to the government. I don't think that's a selfish thing to fight for. What did the letter say?

THOMAS SCOTT: Just that you're on your way and you are thrilled to meet her.

LOUIS RIEL: *I'm* thrilled to meet her?

THOMAS SCOTT: Yeah, I may have signed the letter in your name, for gravitas and such. In retrospect I regret it because I actually find her very charming, even if she is partially a savage. But she's expecting you, not me. And I really think she may be able to help your cause.

LOUIS RIEL: . . . Why are *you* helping my cause? It doesn't benefit you.

THOMAS SCOTT: Because we're friends.

LOUIS RIEL: We're not friends, Thomas. We're just people who hang out sometimes. You're a racist Irish Protestant. I'm a Métis Catholic.

THOMAS SCOTT: So? We're like those dudes from *The Fox and the Hound*. One was a fox and one was a hound and they were different, but they were still friends.

LOUIS RIEL: Yeah, until they grew up.

THOMAS SCOTT: What happened when they grew up?

LOUIS RIEL: Didn't you watch the movie?

THOMAS SCOTT: Well part of it. It was late. I fell asleep. Point is, we all want the same thing, don't we? Freedom, safety, a place to call home.

LOUIS RIEL: I don't know if this country is big enough for all of us. The Reddish River is my home. I am going back to mine . . . I suggest you return to yours.

THOMAS SCOTT: To Ireland? I can't. There's nothing left there.

LOUIS RIEL: Then you understand what I'm fighting for. You don't belong here.

THOMAS SCOTT: And why do you get to make the rules?

LOUIS RIEL: Someone has to. Someone has to stand up to this "Canada" and to John A. Macdonald and to William McDougall . . . and to you.

THOMAS SCOTT: They're Scottish. I'm nothing like them.

LOUIS RIEL: Prove it. Declare, publicly, whose side you're on. Demand restitution. Demand action. Stand up to those people who you say you're nothing like.

*Silence.*

THOMAS SCOTT: . . . I don't see how that would help.

LOUIS RIEL: Hm. Right. Right. The Reddish River will never be your home, Thomas. It is ours. And we won't let you take it away from us. *Au revoir*, my friend. See you on the battlefield.

*LOUIS exits. THOMAS begins to write another letter.*

THOMAS SCOTT: "Dear Prime Minister Macdonald,

Louis Riel is on his way to Reddish River. He plans to lead the next rebellion. Send every support you can. We must do what is right and free Canada from the Indian problem. They refuse to make way for expansion . . . and refuse to make way for the future. And we are the future. And we will prevail. Throbbingly—no—Sincerely, Thomas Scott. Xoxo. No. Just Thomas Scott. Period."

*THOMAS SCOTT seals up the letter and ships it via FedEx.*

# NINE

*The fort.*

**MARIE-ANGELIQUE:** Someone will come. Louis Riel will come. I know he will. If not for me, then for Reddish River. He will seize the fort and will burn this whole place to the ground and then we will be free.

**EUGENIA:** Or dead.

**MARIE-ANGELIQUE:** I'd rather be dead than stuck in here. Don't worry, Eugenia, soon we will be under the magnanimous rule of a great, handsome Métis leader who will protect our way of life and ensure that white settlers and Ottawa surveyors and their docile, useless wives / do not scorch this scared land!

**CECILIA:** Hold on, what the hell are you—

*CECILIA stands, then coughs, then sits.*

**MARIE-ANGELIQUE:** No offence. Soon we will be free. Soon Louis Riel will return.

**CECILIA:** But if he has come to seize the fort . . . what about my husband? My children? What about me?

**MARIE-ANGELIQUE:** What about you? Why is everything always about you?

**CECILIA:** It isn't! But we're people too. What will he do to us in the name of protecting you?

**MARIE-ANGELIQUE:** I don't know.

**EUGENIA:** The rebellion is making a list of rights to protect the land. He intends to create a provisional government.

**CECILIA:** What's that?

**MARIE-ANGELIQUE:** A government just for Reddish River. A government separate from Canada rule and separate from that mouth-breather John A. Macdonald!

**CECILIA:** So, we will all be separated?

**MARIE-ANGELIQUE:** . . . Maybe? I don't know.

*CECILIA coughs several times, more strenuously now.*

You should go to a doctor.

**CECILIA:** I can't go to a doctor. We're trapped here.

**MARIE-ANGELIQUE:** Louis Riel will rescue us.

**CECILIA:** And then divide us. We don't need more division and separation; we need to come together and stop dwelling on the past. Did you learn nothing from your mother?

**MARIE-ANGELIQUE:** Ugh my mother.

**CECILIA:** We are just women. Politics is none of our business.

**MARIE-ANGELIQUE:** But it is! It is our business. These are our lives. And now Ottawa has sent surveyors here to take our land away and claim it for their own. This is what the Canadian Party wants. This is what your husband wants, what Thomas Scott wants, what most of these men on this stupid wall want. And honestly? It sort of sounds like what you want too.

CECILIA: I just don't want to live in fear for my life all the time.

EUGENIA: Yeah, that'd be nice.

CECILIA: Has Ottawa really sent a surveyor?

EUGENIA: The land won't measure up itself.

MARIE-ANGELIQUE: They'll probably do it in squares too. Ugh.

CECILIA: What's wrong with squares?

MARIE-ANGELIQUE: The French do it properly. Seigneurially.

CECILIA: What's that?

EUGENIA: It's a bougie way of saying rectangle.

CECILIA: Surely there is a fair way to lay claim to the free land. If you legally obtain a title to a plot, what reason could they have to take that away? Just divide it all in equal parts and—

MARIE-ANGELIQUE: This is the earth, Cecilia, not a cake. The idea that you can just own a piece of it is so freaking . . . wh*te.

CECILIA: Must we resort to name-calling? You keep implying that I'm racist when clearly you're actually the one racist towards me.

EUGENIA: No, that's not a thing.

CECILIA: We're all just people. Who cares where we come from or what colour our skin is? I don't see myself as white, just like I don't see you as brownish or you as fairly pale but with a summer tan. Besides, your father is white.

MARIE-ANGELIQUE: So what?

CECILIA: So, this is part of your culture, too. You benefit from the same things I benefit from. You purposely choose to separate yourself and draw attention to yourself, but you could choose otherwise. You could choose safety; you could be like me. Stay quiet, stay out of the way, and this will all just blow over. You can get married, and have children, and we can be friends forever, like we always planned.

*CECILIA holds out her pinky.*

MARIE-ANGELIQUE: I can't. I stand with Louis Riel. I stand with the Métis people. I publicly denounce the survey and the theft of our land. I demand retribution for all of us and I will be on the battlefields of the rebellion alongside my people.

*CECILIA drops her pinky.*

CECILIA: Well. At least I still have a friend in Eugenia.

EUGENIA: Uummmmmmhmmm. As much as it pains me to say so since I don't particularly respect him . . . I too stand with Louis Riel.

CECILIA: Oh. Wonderful. This is just fantastic.

MARIE-ANGELIQUE: Cecilia, be our friend. Support us. Speak to your husband. Fight with us.

CECILIA: I care about you both so much. I want us all to be safe and free. And so . . . and so . . . and so . . . and so I support you both but shall refrain from making a decision either way until I better understand the situation.

MARIE-ANGELIQUE: Until you better benefit from a side, you mean.

CECILIA: These are treacherous times. We all must do what it takes to survive.

*No talking. No rocking. A letter arrives and falls in CECILIA's lap.*
*She opens it. She reads it. She closes it.*

Hm. It is from my husband. Louis Riel has been declared leader of the provisional government.

MARIE-ANGELIQUE: Yes! I knew it!

CECILIA: And William McDougall has been declared first lieu-tenant-governor of the territory.

MARIE-ANGELIQUE: Frick.

CECILIA: What does this mean for us?

MARIE-ANGELIQUE: There is no us. Not anymore.

EUGENIA: McDougall is an expansionist. He plans to marginalize the influence of the Métis and the Natives to get what he wants.

MARIE-ANGELIQUE: Land.

EUGENIA: Power.

MARIE-ANGELIQUE: What's the difference?

CECILIA: Maybe he just wants to do what he believes is right.

EUGENIA: He's going to kill us.

*CECILIA gasps.*

MARIE-ANGELIQUE: She means her and I, not you.

CECILIA: Yes, I realize that. I was exhibiting care about your fate. For some reason.

MARIE-ANGELIQUE: I can't let this happen, Eugenia. It would break my mother's heart. This isn't what she fought for. This isn't why she sent me here and left me behind. We must find a way out of this room. Surely there has to be another door. Or a window. There must be something behind all these portraits . . . Behind all these men. Help me find it.

EUGENIA: Okay.

MARIE-ANGELIQUE: Cecilia?

CECILIA: Shan't. It's impossible. I have work to do.

*CECILIA begins to make a new doll.*

*The portraits of the men begin to moan and wail. A baby begins to cry. The triangle dings and dings.*

*MARIE-ANGELIQUE steps closer to the wall. She reaches her hand up and caresses a portrait of someone. The portrait smiles. She leans in, as if to kiss it. Then she rips its head off and holds it in her hand. The portrait blinks. A scream forms on its face but no sound comes out. She eats the head and continues ripping portraits off the wall.*

*After a few moments, EUGENIA joins.*

You're going to ruin everything.

*When the last two portraits—those of THOMAS SCOTT and LOUIS RIEL—are the only ones remaining, a window is revealed. Beyond the window is something similar to a silent night, illuminated by only the moon and a handful of stars. But it's not night and it's not really outside.*

EUGENIA: You first. I've seen it before.

*MARIE-ANGELIQUE climbs through the window. Behind her, it slams shut and disappears.*

# TEN

**MARIE-ANGELIQUE:** Eugenia? Eugenia!

*MARIE-ANGELIQUE pounds on the wall that was once a window. Behind her, THOMAS SCOTT appears.*

**THOMAS SCOTT:** Excuse me, miss.

**MARIE-ANGELIQUE:** Ahh! Stand back, I've got a gun!

*MARIE-ANGELIQUE picks up a stick and waves it around.*

**THOMAS SCOTT:** I think that's a stick.

**MARIE-ANGELIQUE:** Yeah. It is. It is, I panicked, I'm sorry. I don't have any money and I'm not worth murdering or kidnapping, nobody would pay for me or come looking for me, so you should probably just go find someone else to do whatever to, okay, sir?

**THOMAS SCOTT:** I don't mean any harm. I'm looking for someone, a woman who lives in this fort.

**MARIE-ANGELIQUE:** Oh, you must mean Cecilia. She's—

**THOMAS SCOTT:** I'm looking for a Marie-Angelique.

**MARIE-ANGELIQUE:** *Pour moi?*

**THOMAS SCOTT:** Possibly. Is that you? Is this your letter?

MARIE-ANGELIQUE: How did you get that? What have you done with Louis Riel? Tell me. Tell me or I'll shoot.

THOMAS SCOTT: That's still just a stick. Look, I just want to find her to talk. I really liked her letters. So, if you know where she is, I would appreciate it if you would let me know.

MARIE-ANGELIQUE: Maybe she's here. But maybe she's confused about why you have those letters and maybe she would appreciate you telling her why you have them.

THOMAS SCOTT: Louis was . . . is . . . a friend of mine. I transcribed his letters for him. Uh, I'm looking for him right now, as a matter of fact, to, uh, return these to him.

MARIE-ANGELIQUE: I'm looking for him too. I have to warn him. The Canadian Party is on its way and they'll kill him if they find him.

THOMAS SCOTT: Oh, that sucks. Um, maybe we can look together.

MARIE-ANGELIQUE: Sure. Okay. I am Marie-Angelique, by the way. I've been exchanging letters with Louis for some time now. I'm his biggest fan and I want to help in any way I can.

THOMAS SCOTT: We'll find him. Trust me.

> THOMAS and MARIE-ANGELIQUE begin to walk. MARIE-ANGELIQUE shivers. THOMAS puts his coat around her.

MARIE-ANGELIQUE: *Merci.* It's colder outside than I thought it would be. I haven't been outside the fort in some time.

THOMAS SCOTT: Is this where you live?

MARIE-ANGELIQUE: *Oui.* In a room with two other women. We each have a rocking chair and a teacup. It's humble but it's home. Or, well, it *was* home. Where's home for you?

THOMAS SCOTT: I . . . don't know. I guess that's sort of what I'm looking for.

MARIE-ANGELIQUE: I feel that. I've never really felt at home here. I was born in the woods but was sent away to learn how to be a proper lady. I'm afraid I'm not a very good one. I have too many opinions and I can't even sew.

THOMAS SCOTT: Opinions are good. Some people don't have any. I didn't, for a long time. Or maybe I did, but they were born from ignorance and not from wisdom.

MARIE-ANGELIQUE: And your new opinions? Are they wise?

THOMAS SCOTT: Not wise but necessary.

MARIE-ANGELIQUE: Right. Right.

> *MARIE-ANGELIQUE trips and stumbles.* THOMAS SCOTT *catches her.*

You look so familiar to me. You're a friend of Louis's?

THOMAS SCOTT: Definitely. Really close friends.

MARIE-ANGELIQUE: I wonder if you were on our wall. There was Louis . . . and Gabriel Dumont . . . and Keanu . . . and Thomas Scott . . . and . . . left side part . . . Thomas Scott. Racist. Irish. Protestant. Thomas Scott. That's you, you're him, you're not a friend, you're an enemy, the worst one, you're a . . . you're a . . .

THOMAS SCOTT: I'm a what?

MARIE-ANGELIQUE: You're going to kill him, aren't you?

THOMAS SCOTT: I'm just following orders.

MARIE-ANGELIQUE: Why?

THOMAS SCOTT: I had to make a choice. We are fighting for the future, Marie-Angelique. We are fighting for a better Canada.

MARIE-ANGELIQUE: Better for who? Because it's certainly not better for him or for me.

> *MARIE-ANGELIQUE takes off THOMAS's jacket, throws it to the ground, and stomps on it.*

THOMAS SCOTT: Hey, that's not cool.

MARIE-ANGELIQUE: You know what isn't cool, Thomas? Genocide.

THOMAS SCOTT: Okay, yeah, I know that. I'm not saying genocide is cool. I'm a good person, Marie-Angelique. I want the same thing you do; I want to find a place where I belong and—

MARIE-ANGELIQUE: Then go back to Ireland, Thomas! Go anywhere else! Why here? Why do you need to take this from us? Why do you need everything?

THOMAS SCOTT: I don't want everything; I just want something. There's nothing here for Irish people either—no jobs, no housing . . . I want a better life, one where I don't have to prove every day I belong here and deserve to be treated with respect.

MARIE-ANGELIQUE: Tell me, Thomas. What's your zodiac sign?

**THOMAS SCOTT:** I don't know.

**MARIE-ANGELIQUE:** What's your date of birth?

**THOMAS SCOTT:** January first.

**MARIE-ANGELIQUE:** A Capricorn. Well. From one fixed Earth sign to another, one that understands your desire for stability, I have to say that although I understand where you're coming from, and although I empathize . . . I expected better from you.

**THOMAS SCOTT:** Maybe that's your problem. Expectations.

**MARIE-ANGELIQUE:** Excsqueeze me?

**THOMAS SCOTT:** What do you expect will happen when you find Louis Riel? Do you think he'll just fall in love with you and rescue you and fix everything? Louis is a delusional coward. He can't lead a rebellion. He can't even write a good poem.

*LOUIS RIEL enters.*

**LOUIS RIEL:** Why don't you say that to my face, Thomas Scott?

**THOMAS SCOTT:** All right, I will, Louis Riel.

**MARIE-ANGELIQUE:** Hi, my name is Marie-Angelique and—

**THOMAS SCOTT:** Your poems are garbage and so are you.

**MARIE-ANGELIQUE:** I actually don't think they're that bad—

**LOUIS RIEL:** You must be the poor girl who has been exchanging letters with the late, great Mr. Scott here, hmm?

MARIE-ANGELIQUE: I what? Ew? Oh. No. Ew. You weren't the
. . . oh yuck.

THOMAS SCOTT: That's very rude. I was being sincere when I said I
really enjoyed talking to you.

LOUIS RIEL: And did you also enjoy the words of our friend Thomas
Scott here, Marie-Angelique? Perhaps it is his side you are really on?

*THOMAS SCOTT and MARIE-ANGELIQUE share a meaningful look.*

MARIE-ANGELIQUE: No. Absolutely not. I fight for the Métis nation, to
protect them from people like you.

LOUIS RIEL: Two against one, old sport. Better just surrender and—

*THOMAS SCOTT grabs MARIE-ANGELIQUE's stick and holds it against
her head.*

THOMAS SCOTT: Come any closer and I'll shoot.

LOUIS RIEL: That's a stick.

THOMAS SCOTT: I'll kill her. I will.

LOUIS RIEL: Why should I care about that?

MARIE-ANGELIQUE: Hey! I just said I was on your side!

LOUIS RIEL: To make a Tomlette you have to crack a few eggs.

THOMAS SCOTT: Terrible joke.

MARIE-ANGELIQUE: Eugenia was right. You're nothing like I thought
you were.

*LOUIS RIEL pauses. He considers this. Then, he picks up a stick.*

**LOUIS RIEL:** Let her go or I'll shoot.

**MARIE-ANGELIQUE:** Okay, so now you both have sticks. That's kind of . . . kind of hot.

*LOUIS RIEL and THOMAS SCOTT get in a stick gun fight. It starts out silly but grows increasingly serious. There's lots of ad libbing. It ends with LOUIS capturing THOMAS. THOMAS drops the stick and MARIE-ANGELIQUE picks it up.*

**LOUIS RIEL:** Come along, Thomas Scott. The time has come for you to die.

**THOMAS SCOTT:** I die with honour. I die with dignity. I die with—

**LOUIS RIEL:** Shh. No more words. Thank you, Marie-Angelique, for all your assistance.

**MARIE-ANGELIQUE:** I didn't really do anything. I just came to warn you that your enemies are coming. Or, rather, that they are already here.

**LOUIS RIEL:** Yes. In many ways Thomas Scott is my enemy . . . but I also believe that the enemy of my enemy is my friend. And we have been friends, haven't we, old sport?

**THOMAS SCOTT:** Well, I—

**LOUIS RIEL:** Shh.

*LOUIS muzzles THOMAS.*

**MARIE-ANGELIQUE:** What else do you believe in?

LOUIS RIEL: I believe in fate. I believe in the land. I believe in the Métis people. I believe in you.

MARIE-ANGELIQUE: I've been waiting for you for so long. My friends and I are trapped in a room in the fort and I've prayed and prayed that you would find us and free us.

LOUIS RIEL: How did you get out here?

MARIE-ANGELIQUE: I climbed through a window.

LOUIS RIEL: That's the only kind of freedom that counts—the kind you make for yourself. We must be off.

MARIE-ANGELIQUE: Take me with you? I can fight.

LOUIS RIEL: I work alone.

MARIE-ANGELIQUE: I'll be quiet. I'll bring snacks.

LOUIS RIEL: I subsist solely on the blood of my enemies.

MARIE-ANGELIQUE: I can accommodate dietary restrictions.

LOUIS RIEL: I have been chosen.

MARIE-ANGELIQUE: By whom?

LOUIS RIEL: God. I am the prophet of the new world. I can hear them now. The bells, the angels. Do you hear them? The footfalls. The horsemen.

*In the distance, voices are heard shouting "Marie-Angelique."*

MARIE-ANGELIQUE: I don't hear anything.

*The voices grow louder.*

**LOUIS RIEL:** You will. The woods are on fire. The sky burns. We are beyond . . . and I am the One. Farewell.

*LOUIS RIEL exits with THOMAS SCOTT. They disappear into the darkness. MARIE-ANGELIQUE begins to walk towards the voices. Suddenly, a gunshot is heard, followed by a scream. She keeps walking. "Marie-Angelique!" Gunshot. Scream. Walking. Again and again. Over and over. Until . . . she finds the window.*

# ELEVEN

*MARIE-ANGELIQUE crawls through the window. It's the same room, the same place, but now there's a breeze . . . and clouds . . . and the moon . . . and hope. And CECILIA has just finished making a new doll.*

**CECILIA:** Finished!

*She hands it to EUGENIA.*

**EUGENIA:** Gabriel Dumont! Aw, you shouldn't have.

*MARIE-ANGELIQUE clears her throat.*

**CECILIA:** Oh! Hello!

**EUGENIA:** Welcome home.

**CECILIA:** We thought you were never coming back.

**MARIE-ANGELIQUE:** How long was I gone?

**CECILIA:** It seemed like forever.

**MARIE-ANGELIQUE:** It felt like a minute. Why did nobody come looking for me?

**CECILIA:** Yours is not the only life at stake. Count your blessings that yours was not a life lost. My husband and Thomas Scott were not so lucky.

EUGENIA: It's not her fault, Cecilia. Louis had to set an example.

CECILIA: With my husband? With Thomas? He was so handsome.

MARIE-ANGELIQUE: He was very handsome, Cecilia, you're right. But Louis had to show the government that we are to be taken seriously.

CECILIA: What will I do without a husband? What will my children do without their father?

MARIE-ANGELIQUE: I'm sorry. I don't know.

CECILIA: What about our pinky swears? What about our pact? What about our friendship?

MARIE-ANGELIQUE: Louis said that sometimes the enemy of our enemy is our friend.

CECILIA: I am your friend, not your enemy.

MARIE-ANGELIQUE: In many ways, you are my enemy. But you shouldn't be. I don't want you to be. And if you believe we all deserve to live peacefully on this land, then you are also my friend.

CECILIA: I do believe that. I do. I don't want to be your enemy either.

MARIE-ANGELIQUE: Then there is work to be done. We must find our own way out . . . no man will save us. We do not need to be saved, but we must keep working. Agreed?

CECILIA: Agreed.

EUGENIA: Agreed. That's kind of what I've been saying the whole time anyway.

*The three women pinky swear and write three new letters.*

Dear Louis,

**MARIE-ANGELIQUE:** Dear Louis,

**CECILIA:** Dear Louis,

**EUGENIA:** Remember the wisdom of your ancestors. Remember the lessons of your forefathers.

**MARIE-ANGELIQUE:** It was so nice to meet you the other day.

**CECILIA:** My name is Cecilia. You murdered my husband. And Thomas Scott, the handsome Irishman.

**MARIE-ANGELIQUE:** I'm embarrassed by what I wrote you before and wish to apologize.

**CECILIA:** But perhaps not everything is quite as it seems.

**EUGENIA:** "Quit your bitchin' and start *miigwitchin*'," an ancient meme.

**MARIE-ANGELIQUE:** I created an idea of you inside my head, and it turned out to be untrue.

**CECILIA:** Perhaps we all want to be safe, and free.

**MARIE-ANGELIQUE:** Maybe you aren't who I thought you were . . . but that's okay. I don't know if I'm who I thought I was either.

**EUGENIA:** It's a funny thing these days . . . nobody seems to know where they belong.

**CECILIA:** Do remember, Louis, as you well know as a devout Catholic, that the Lord will have the final say.

**EUGENIA:** Even the muskrats are confused and don't know where to go.

**MARIE-ANGELIQUE:** I did not always live in this fort. I was born in the woods. I loved the woods. And then my mother, she . . . I couldn't forgive her for what she did.

**CECILIA:** Don't become so involved with the details that you can no longer see the forest for the trees.

**MARIE-ANGELIQUE:** I thought it was a choice. I couldn't forgive her for letting them take me.

**EUGENIA:** But I'm rooting for ya, old sport. And it wasn't you. It was me. I promise.

**MARIE-ANGELIQUE:** Fight for us, Louis. Keep fighting and don't ever stop. I'll join you when I can. I'll find my own way out. Whether that's tomorrow or a hundred years from now.

**CECILIA:** Evil is inevitable. But us women of the fur trade are indefatigable.

**EUGENIA:** Throbbingly yours, your platonic friend, Eugenia.

**CECILIA:** Curtly but daintily, Cecilia.

**MARIE-ANGELIQUE:** Sincerely, Marie-Angelique.

> *The three women seal up their letters and toss them high in the air.*
> *CECILIA begins to cough.*

**EUGENIA:** Oh, Cecilia . . .

**CECILIA:** Nothing serious. Don't worry about me. I have always been happy here in the fort. But, Eugenia, we must find a way out so you can return to work.

**EUGENIA:** No more, not for me. I am older now . . . the animals can hear me coming a mile away. My bones creak, my muscles ache . . . I believe I shall stay here, and grow old, and return to the earth peacefully when the time comes.

MARIE-ANGELIQUE: But that time is far away! We are still young yet. There is so much to do. So much is possible. Cecilia, might we all have some tea?

CECILIA: There is no tea. There was never any tea. The tea was a lie.

*And a letter falls from the sky again and into* EUGENIA's *lap.*

EUGENIA: A letter.

CECILIA: From?

EUGENIA: One guess.

ALL: Louis Riel.

LOUIS RIEL: Dear Women of the Fur Trade,

Thank you for your letters. I was ever so pleased to hear from all of you and would like to inform you that, yes, it is I writing this. It was even wonderful to hear from you, Eugenia, who broke my heart so many years ago. It has been so long since we last made sweet, sweet love on the banks of the River Red where the beaver makes its nest and the children frolic innocently amongst the tall grasses and the wood ticks. So much has changed, Eugenia. I've changed. I am married now. My wife, Marguerite, so hot, and I love her an appropriate amount for the time period. And I have children, Jean-Louis and Marie-Angelique—truly a beautiful name, inspired by one of my greatest fans—

*MARIE-ANGELIQUE smiles.*

—the loves of my life, after rebellion, resistance, and destroying the lives of the colonizers of our land. A close fourth place for my focus and attention. I will keep fighting, as you requested. And I await all of your faces, and all of your strength, on the battlefield beside me. RIEL OUT.

EUGENIA: There will be a rebellion west of us now. The territories there saw what Louis Riel did for us. Now they demand the same from him, for themselves.

MARIE-ANGELIQUE: He succeeded here, and he will succeed out west. With our help he cannot fail.

EUGENIA: I imagine he will petition the government. He will outline the grievances and neglect the territories continue to suffer in this fight between the Indians, the Métis, and the settlers.

MARIE-ANGELIQUE: Fuck the settlers.

*CECILIA coughs.*

MARIE-ANGELIQUE: Oh gosh, sorry. Sorry. The enemy of my enemy is my friend, pinky swear, all that, yes.

EUGENIA: The settlers are important. The government will listen to their concerns. They won't listen to ours. It was foolish to believe they ever would. Louis will need the support of all of us and all of our communities. Ottawa has disrespected our treaty agreements, and stolen our bannock recipes, and wears our regalia as Halloween costumes. I cannot abide any of it. I will send word home.

MARIE-ANGELIQUE: As will I.

CECILIA: As will I.

*The three women pen their last three letters, ever. I promise.*

Dear Mother,

EUGENIA: Dear Mother,

MARIE-ANGELIQUE: Dear Mother,

CECILIA: I am writing to you about a matter of dire importance.

MARIE-ANGELIQUE: My name is Marie-Angelique, and I am your daughter.

EUGENIA: To whomever is reading this, please read it aloud.

CECILIA: My friends and I need our family's help.

MARIE-ANGELIQUE: Do you even remember me?

EUGENIA: I am losing our language and can only communicate in English now.

CECILIA: We are trapped in a fort, and they are losing their land, and their people are dying at our own hands.

MARIE-ANGELIQUE: The last memory I have of you was your turned back as they took me away.

EUGENIA: That's what you get for spending too much time in the forts. Tell my mother we require help.

CECILIA: Dying at your hands, and the hands of our people.

MARIE-ANGELIQUE: Did you not want me? Or was this your way of giving me a better life?

CECILIA: But I am not here for shame or guilt. The Lord will have his way. Justice will be swift with those who betray God and his nations.

**MARIE-ANGELIQUE:** I didn't need a better life. I needed my family. A man named Louis Riel . . .

**EUGENIA:** He is fighting for us.

**CECILIA:** I urge you to reconsider your position and send aid. If not for them, then for me, your daughter, as I am very ill, and my time here is limited. And in that limited time, my deepest wish is for I and my friends to be free.

**MARIE-ANGELIQUE:** He is fighting for us. So that mothers will never again have to give up their children. So that we may all grow up on healthy land with healthy spirits.

**ALL:** Rally those you can. Please send them here.

**EUGENIA:** Eugenia.

**CECILIA:** Cecilia.

**MARIE-ANGELIQUE:** Marie-Angelique.

*The three women seal up their three letters and toss them into the air for the last time. As they do, dozens of letters fall from the sky, like snowflakes or raindrops. MARIE-ANGELIQUE picks up a letter and reads it.*

Louis Riel has petitioned the Canadian government, to no avail.

*CECILIA picks up a letter and reads it.*

**CECILIA:** His tactics have grown militant and aggressive and is surely not to be tolerated much longer.

*EUGENIA picks up a letter and reads it.*

**EUGENIA:** His mind deteriorates.

*CECILIA picks up a letter and reads it.*

**CECILIA:** He has visions.

*MARIE-ANGELIQUE picks up a letter and reads it.*

**MARIE-ANGELIQUE:** He believes himself to be a prophet.

*EUGENIA picks up a letter and reads it.*

**EUGENIA:** Armed conflict in Saskatchewan.

*CECILIA picks up a letter and reads it.*

**CECILIA:** The settlers have revoked their support.

*MARIE-ANGELIQUE picks up a letter and reads it.*

**MARIE-ANGELIQUE:** The Métis troops have been defeated by the government.

*EUGENIA picks up a letter and reads it.*

**EUGENIA:** Louis Riel has been arrested.

*CECILIA picks up a letter and reads it.*

**CECILIA:** Ottawa demands his execution.

*EUGENIA picks up a letter and reads it.*

**EUGENIA:** Guilty.

**MARIE-ANGELIQUE:** A retrial. He must demand a retrial.

*CECILIA picks up a letter and reads it.*

CECILIA: Denied.

EUGENIA: "He shall die though every dog in Quebec bark in his favour."

*A full moon—a red moon—appears low in the sky. The women howl at it like dogs. Its light directs them to this spot, here and now, where the nation's biggest celebrity is about to meet their fate. Today is the day that LOUIS RIEL dies, but today is just the beginning.*

# TWELVE

*CECILIA, EUGENIA, and MARIE-ANGELIQUE kneel to pray. They each make the sign of the cross. EUGENIA does this badly.*

CECILIA: In the name of the Father, the Son, and the Holy Ghost.

MARIE-ANGELIQUE: Are you there, God? It's me, Marie-Angelique.

EUGENIA: Sup.

CECILIA: I pray for your divine forgiveness.

MARIE-ANGELIQUE: I don't know if you're real, but . . .

EUGENIA: Um, do I just ask you for what I want?

CECILIA: On behalf of myself, my husband, and Louis Riel.

MARIE-ANGELIQUE: I endeavour to be prime minister now, a person with purpose, not merely the wife of a purposeful man.

EUGENIA: Is that how this works?

MARIE-ANGELIQUE: I ask for your help, if you are there. If you're listening.

CECILIA: I feel weaker every day, but I shall not waste prayers on myself.

MARIE-ANGELIQUE: Please let Louis through the gates and into heaven, if that's a thing you do.

EUGENIA: I want you to be nice to my friend Louis. He's done some real dope shit. I think you'd be proud, if you're . . . well, I don't know your political affiliations / so . . .

MARIE-ANGELIQUE: He has a good heart, and a noble mind.

CECILIA: I pray for the divine forgiveness of my husband and the forgiveness of my friends.

MARIE-ANGELIQUE: I shall never forgive our oppressors.

EUGENIA: Forgiveness is not ours to give.

MARIE-ANGELIQUE: I'd like to ask you about rigging elections.

CECILIA: And a final prayer for Louis Riel.

MARIE-ANGELIQUE: But this seems like the wrong time.

EUGENIA: He is on his journey home.

| CECILIA: A final prayer For all our heroes A prayer For a disappearing people A prayer For a dying way of life. | EUGENIA: A final prayer For all our heroes A prayer For a disappearing people A prayer For a dying way of life. | MARIE-ANGELIQUE: A final prayer For all our heroes A prayer For a disappearing people A prayer For a dying way of life. |
|---|---|---|

*LOUIS RIEL walks to the gallows. He holds a silver cross in his hand. His hair has been shaved. His face is calm . . . amused, even. He is adored and he is despised. He is a hero and a villain. He is everything to everyone. The three women watch.*

CECILIA: The Lord is my shepherd; I shall not want. He maketh me to lie down in green pastures: he leadeth me beside the still waters. He restoreth my soul.

*Hesitantly, MARIE-ANGELIQUE joins CECILIA and holds her hand.*

CECILIA & MARIE-ANGELIQUE: He leadeth me in the paths of righteousness for his name's sake. Yea, though I walk through the valley of the shadow of death, I will fear no—

*LOUIS RIEL is hanged. EUGENIA grabs their hands but does not join in the prayer.*

. . . evil: for thou art with me; thy rod and thy staff they comfort me.

*His body twitches.*

Thou preparest a table before me in the presence of mine enemies . . .

*The rope creaks and groans.*

Thou anointest my head with oil.

*It sways back and forth.*

My cup runneth over.

*And back and forth.*

Surely goodness and mercy shall follow me all the days of my life.

*And back and forth . . .*

And I will dwell in the house of the Lord . . .

> *. . . until coming to a gentle stop.*

. . . forever.

> *Some time passes.*

EUGENIA: And the People Were Crying.

MARIE-ANGELIQUE: And the Sun Was Shining.

CECILIA: The Frost Made Everything Glitter, Like Diamonds.

EUGENIA: Last Words:

LOUIS RIEL: Mr. John A. Macdonald, I send you a message. I have not the honour to know you personally . . . Do not let yourself be completely carried away by the glories of power.

CECILIA: His face looked calm before they covered it with the white cap.

EUGENIA: He held a silver crucifix in his hand and kissed it.

MARIE-ANGELIQUE: What was it for? What was his purpose?

EUGENIA: All things have a purpose. These animals, for instance. They weren't going around wondering what their purpose was. They were just living. And in that life, fulfilling their purpose. They keep us warm, and fed. Cycles. Their lives end, but their purpose continues on long after they've been forgotten.

MARIE-ANGELIQUE: I don't want to be forgotten. I still want to do something important.

EUGENIA: Me too.

CECILIA: Me too.

*A long, sad pause.*

What shall we do now?

MARIE-ANGELIQUE: Well. We could go get furs.

> *The wind blows. The sky is cloudy and full of tears. The rain falls gently and steadily. It mixes with the green grass and makes the ground soft and muddy.*
>
> *The women walk solemnly in straight lines to the gentle sound of a funeral march. Frost covers the tips of their eyelashes and nips at their bare faces. The ground is snow and mud. Their feet get dirtier and dirtier with each step. They come to a stop in front of a six-foot-wide hole in the ground that has opened up like a hungry mouth—the final resting place of LOUIS RIEL.*
>
> *The women watch as his casket is lowered into the earth. The women leave flowers on his grave.*
>
> *They each light a candle and return to their rocking chairs in their room in the fort. They never really left. They were always there.*

# THIRTEEN

*They rock back and forth and back and forth and back and forth. The water boils. The baby cries. The gunshots blare. The horses gallop. There are too many sounds.*

**MARIE-ANGELIQUE:** "I know that through the grace of God, / I am the founder of Manitoba."

**CECILIA:** "We must cherish our inheritance. We must preserve / our nationality for the youth of our future. The story should be written down to pass on."

*CECILIA begins to cough.*

**EUGENIA:** "Deeds are not accomplished in a few days, or in a few hours. / A century is only a spoke in the wheel of everlasting time."

**MARIE-ANGELIQUE:** "I am more convinced every day that without a single exception I did right. And I have always believed that, as I have acted / honestly, the time will come when the people of Canada will see and acknowledge it."

**CECILIA:** "I have nothing but my heart and I have given it long ago to my country."

*CECILIA stops coughing and falls asleep.*

**EUGENIA:** "In a little while it will be over. We may fail. But the rights / for which we contend will not die."

*EUGENIA falls asleep.*

**MARIE-ANGELIQUE:** "My people will sleep for one hundred years, but when they awake, it will be the artists who give them their spirit back."

*MARIE-ANGELIQUE falls asleep.*

*The women sleep for one hundred years, holding their dolls in their arms.*

*And the fort falls apart around them.*

*The end.*

# ACKNOWLEDGEMENTS

There are probably a lot of people I should acknowledge here, because that is the respectful thing to do. Days before writing this acknowledgement, I read that you should keep an ongoing list of all the people you need to acknowledge. I wish I had read that sooner. Alas, I kept no such list, and so I would like to take over this section and turn it into an apology section, where I humbly beg for forgiveness for all the people I have forgotten to acknowledge. Besties, your contributions were legit unforgettable.

Frances Koncan is a writer of mixed Anishinaabe and Slovene descent from Couchiching First Nation in Treaty 3 territory, and currently living and working on Treaty 1 territory in Winnipeg, Manitoba. She learned to write by fighting with adults on the Internet in the late '90s before Internet safety was a consideration. Their theatrical career began in 2007 when they saw a production of *The Threepenny Opera* starring Alan Cumming and he accidently touched her shoulder. In her free time, she likes playing video games and adding expensive luxury goods to her online shopping cart with no intention of ever checking out.

First edition: June 2022
Printed and bound in Canada by Rapido Books, Montreal

Cover artwork by Christi Belcourt. *Untitled*, 1997, private collection of
Alanis Obomsawin.
Author photo © Ady Kay Photography

**PLAYWRIGHTS
CANADA PRESS**

202-269 Richmond St. W.
Toronto, ON
M5V 1X1

416.703.0013
info@playwrightscanada.com
www.playwrightscanada.com
@playcanpress